JOANNA COLE
AN INSECT'S BODY

photographs by
Jerome Wexler and Raymond A. Mendez

William Morrow and Company
New York   1984

For reading and commenting on the manuscript, the author thanks
Dr. Thomas J. Walker, Professor of Entomology, University of Florida, and
Dr. Richard Alexander, Professor of Entomology, University of Michigan.
Thanks also to Dr. James Nation, Professor of Entomology, University of
Florida, for providing help with text and illustration on the digestive system
of the house cricket.

Author's note: The insect shown in this book is the common European
house cricket, the original "cricket on the hearth."

Picture Credits   Photographs on pages 4, 8, 10, 15, 19, 22, 25, 26, 27, 28, 29, 30, 31, 33, and 45 by Jerome
Wexler. All other photographs by Raymond A. Mendez.

Printed in the United States of America.

10 9 8 7 6 5 4 3

Library of Congress Cataloging in Publication Data
Cole, Joanna. An insect's body.
Summary: Examines the common house cricket and shows why its body is ideally suited for
survival.   1. Crickets—Juvenile literature. [1. Crickets] I. Wexler, Jerome, ill. II. Mendez, Raymond
A., ill. III. Title. QL508.G8C65 1984   595.7'26   83-22027
ISBN 0-688-02771-7
ISBN 0-688-02772-5 (lib. bdg.)

Book design by Cindy Simon

To Michael Stone

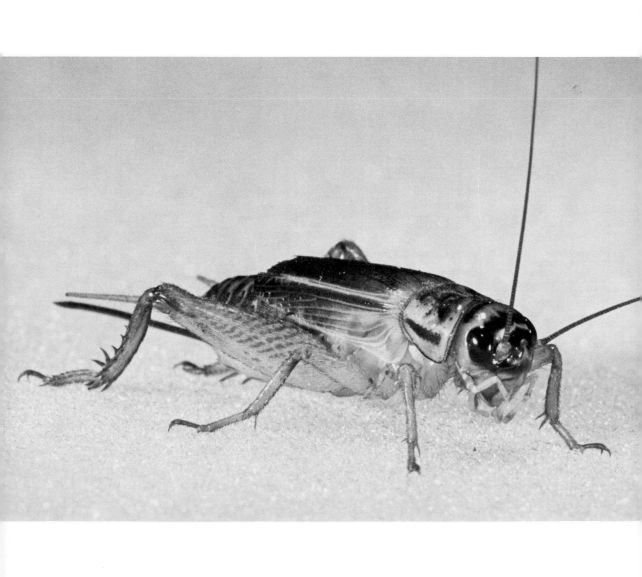

With their large eyes and waving feelers, insects may seem more like creatures from another planet than earthlings like ourselves. Yet these alien-looking animals have the same need for food, water, and oxygen as we do. And in order to survive, they must have nerves, muscles, and the ability to produce young.

Their numbers show that they are very good at survival: There are four times as many insects as all other animals put together!

If we look closely at a single, ordinary insect—a common house cricket—we can see how its body helps it survive.

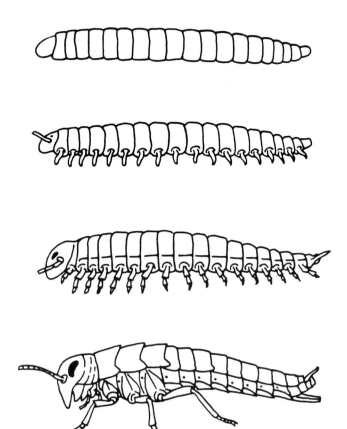

Scientists think the ancestor of all insects was a pre-
historic worm. Its body was made up of many
segments, or sections.

As millions of years passed, the descendants of this
animal became less and less like worms. They evolved
legs, and groups of the segments joined together, or
fused, to form three main body parts.

Today, different kinds of insects look very different from each other. But every insect has six legs, and its body is divided into three parts.

The first section is the head, which contains a tiny brain connected by nerves to the eyes, antennae or feelers, and the mouthparts.

The middle section—the thorax—is the insect's locomotion center. It always bears three pairs of legs and, usually, two pairs of wings.

The rear section—the abdomen—carries the organs for digesting food, breathing, mating, and in females, laying eggs.

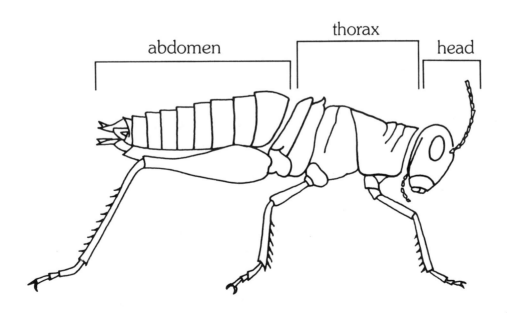

abdomen   thorax   head

Every animal needs water to live and must have a way of keeping its body from drying out. Most very small animals live right in the water, and those that live on land usually stay in moist places. For example, an earthworm, with its soft, moist skin, needs to stay underground in damp earth to survive.

Insects, however, can live almost anywhere. This is because an insect's body is covered with a tough, waterproof suit of armor.

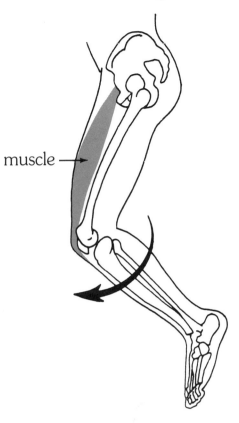

Human Leg

muscle →

The covering is called an exoskeleton, which means outside skeleton. Made of a material similar to our fingernails, this hard shell supports an insect's body just like the bones inside our body. And just as our muscles move our limbs by pulling against our bones, the insect's tiny muscles are attached to the inside of the exoskeleton at flexible joints.

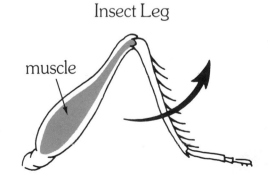

Insect Leg

muscle

9

Even if we knew nothing about how crickets move, we would be able to tell a lot just from looking at their hind legs. The very large thigh muscles—similar to those of a frog or a grasshopper—tell us that these are jumping legs.

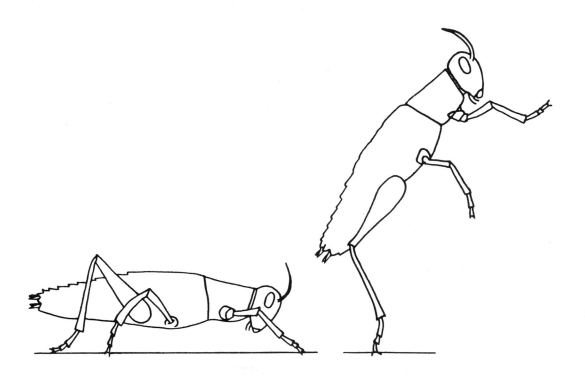

Thigh muscles tighten   *Foot pushes against ground*

When the thigh muscles tighten, they pull back on the knee joints, which swing the lower legs back. Instead of kicking backward, however, the lower legs are held in place by the claws and spines on the feet, which grip the ground. Since the feet are anchored, the force of the muscles pushes the insect's entire body up and forward in the typical cricket's leap.

A cricket can jump more than twenty times the length
of its own body.

If humans had the same ability, an average man or woman could leap thirty feet in a single bound.

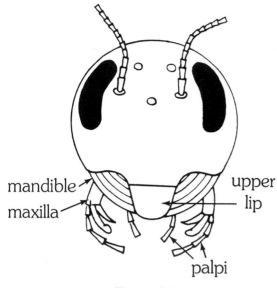

mandible
maxilla
upper lip
palpi

Front View

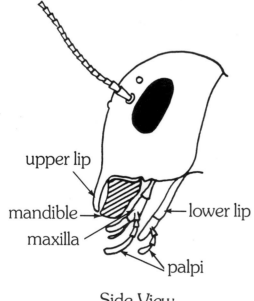

upper lip
mandible
maxilla
lower lip
palpi

Side View

Food is the fuel that animals use to power their bodies. Some insects eat vegetable food, others prefer animal food. House crickets have a chewing mouth and eat both kinds.

A cricket's mouth is nothing but a hole at the front of its head. This opening is surrounded by mouthparts, which form a kind of Swiss army knife to perform all the functions needed for eating.

Behind a flat upper lip, two biting jaws called mandibles open and close sideways like tongs to cut food into bite-size pieces. Behind these, a smaller pair of jaws called maxillae pass food into the mouth.

14

Another part forms a lower lip, and inside this is the cricket's tongue. The organs of taste are found not on the tongue, but on the maxillae and on the jointed palpi that hang down in front. If the palpi look like legs, this is because they and most of the other mouthparts *were* legs in the insects' many-legged ancestors. Over time, the legs near the head evolved into eating utensils.

Digestive System

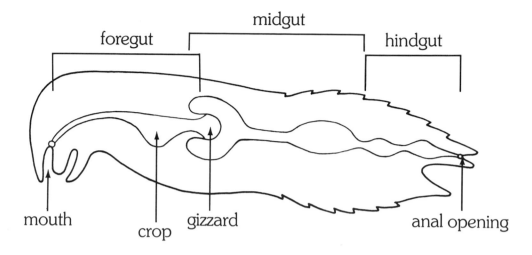

The cricket's food moves through the sections of its gut as it is digested. First the food goes to the crop, where it is mixed with saliva. Next it is ground up into smaller pieces by the gizzard. From there it passes to the midgut, where digestive juices break it down into nutrients that can be used by the body. Any parts of the food that cannot be digested end up in the hindgut and are disposed of as waste.

Nutrients pass right through the walls of the midgut into the abdomen, which is filled with blood. Unlike our own blood, which flows through blood vessels, an insect's blood sloshes about in the spaces around the internal organs.

16

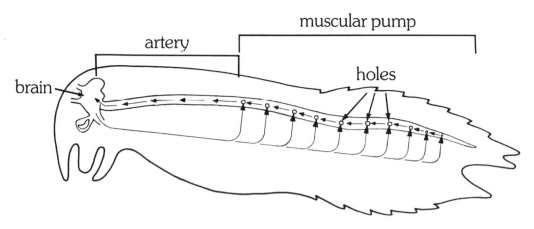

Circulatory system

muscular pump

artery

holes

brain

Arrows show how blood flows through an insect's body.

The insect's heart is a hollow tube. The rear part is a muscular pump with several holes along the sides. The front part is a long artery leading to the head. The pump draws in blood through the side holes and pushes it up through the tube. The blood pours out and over the brain. Then it oozes back through the midsection and eventually flows to the abdomen again.

This simple circulation of the blood is almost like stirring. With a few extra pumps to push blood into the narrow legs and antennae, the system is efficient enough to bring food molecules to the cells of the muscles, organs, and other parts of a tiny animal like an insect.

Surprisingly, an insect's blood is not red like ours. The red blood you see when you swat a mosquito is actually its food, drawn from the person or animal it has just bitten.

The insect's own blood is a yellowish color. This is because it does not have the special red oxygen carrier—hemoglobin—that in higher animals brings oxygen from the lungs to all parts of the body.

blood

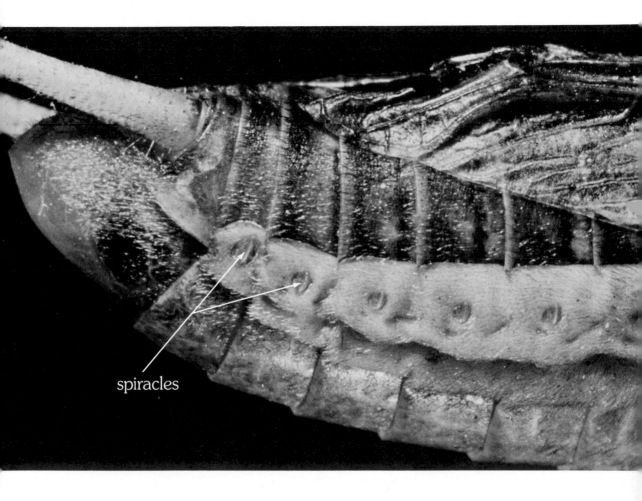

spiracles

  Insects do not have lungs, and oxygen does not travel
in their blood. Instead, air enters the body through
breathing holes, or spiracles, on the insect's sides. These
openings lead to tiny air tubes, which carry oxygen to
every cell in the insect's small body. Animals need
oxygen to convert food into energy.

Air-tube System

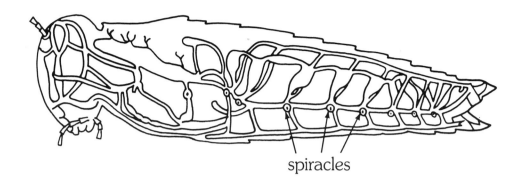

spiracles

Nervous System

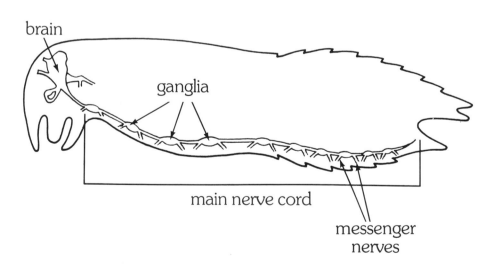

brain

ganglia

main nerve cord

messenger nerves

To survive, an insect needs a nervous system to receive information about the world and to control its body. The nervous system has several parts: a simple brain in the head; a main nerve cord that runs from the brain to the abdomen; messenger nerves that connect the limbs and sense organs to the brain and nerve cord; and ganglia—knotlike bunches of nerve cells that lie along the nerve cord. Each of the ganglia acts as an "assistant brain."

Because of these assistant brains, many insects can live for quite a while after their heads have been cut off. A praying mantis can even mate without a head, and a headless cricket can chirp! This is because the ganglia, rather than the main brain, control these actions.

It may look as if the cricket has two eyes, but it really has several hundred. Like most other insects, the cricket's large eyes on the sides of its head are actually compound eyes. This means they are made up of many individual eyes called facets.

An insect's eyes cannot move or focus on objects the way our eyes do. Instead, each facet gets an image of a little piece of the surroundings, and together these pieces make a picture of the whole. While a cricket probably cannot see very sharply, its compound eyes are especially good for detecting movement, since a moving object will appear quickly in one facet after another.

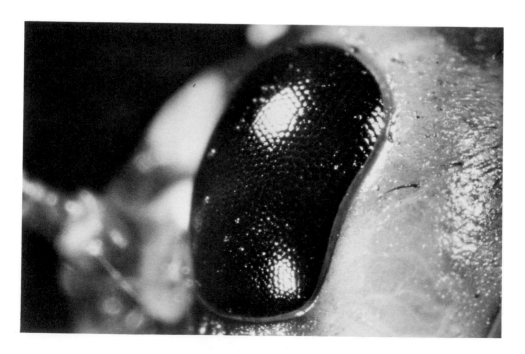

In addition to the compound eyes, there are three simple eyes on top of the head. The insect cannot see with the simple eyes alone, but they seem to serve as boosters to make the compound eyes more sensitive to light.

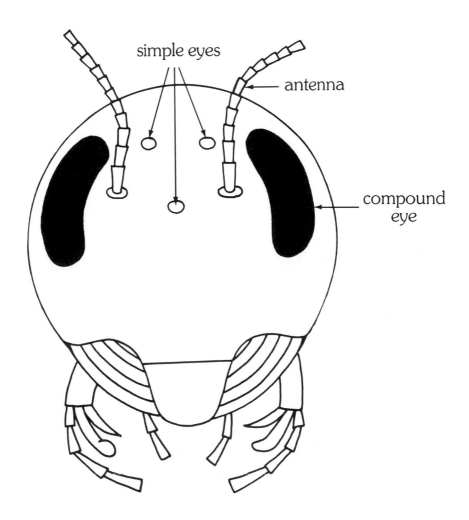

simple eyes

antenna

compound eye

24

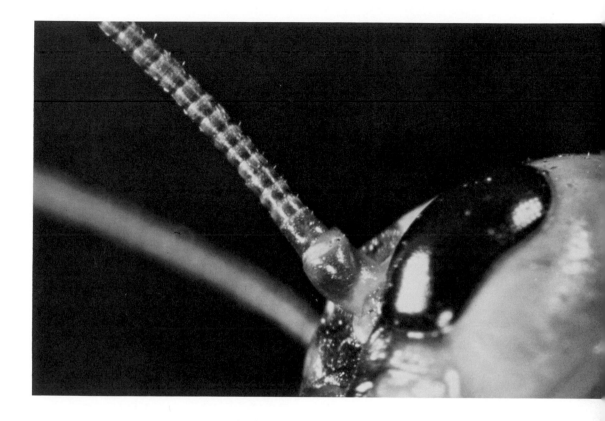

Just as important to an insect as its eyes are its jointed feelers, or antennae. The antennae look simple, but they are actually the insect's most complicated sense organs. They are covered with thousands of tiny bristles and pegs. Some of these detect air movements, others can tell whether the air is dry or damp, some pick up sounds, but most are organs of smell. In a way, the antennae are an insect's nose.

Close-up photographs show that a cricket's body is covered with hairs. These are not for keeping the insect warm, however. They are sense organs attached to nerve cells inside the armor. They respond mostly to touch, but also to air and sound waves.

A cricket has 750 of these hairs on each of its rear feelers. If you have ever tried to grab a cricket from behind, you know how fast they can detect air currents made by your hand. The escape message usually gets to the jumping muscles before you get to the cricket.

If you see a cricket in a position like this, don't think it's doing its exercises. It is actually taking a bath. With its mouth, it is cleaning off the sensitive hairs that are so important to its survival.

Crickets have ears, but they are in a surprising place. Just below the "knee" joint on each foreleg is a smooth patch with an air space beneath the surface. This is the cricket's eardrum.

Crickets need good hearing because they "talk" to each other with sounds. Most other insects have no ears. Moths communicate with their sense of smell, and fireflies signal each other with light, but crickets send messages by chirping.

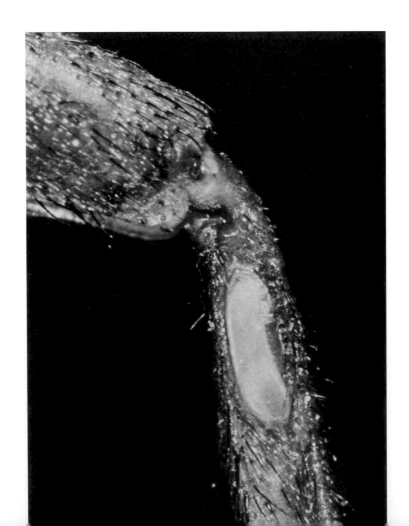

When people hear crickets chirping on a summer night, the sound seems cheerful. Of course, there is no way of knowing how cricket feels when it is singing, but we do know that the song is not sung purely for joy. It serves the very practical purpose of attracting a mate.

Only male crickets sing—not females—and they don't do it with their mouths, nor do they rub their legs together, as many people think. Crickets sing by raising their wings and moving them briskly across each other, like opening and closing scissors.

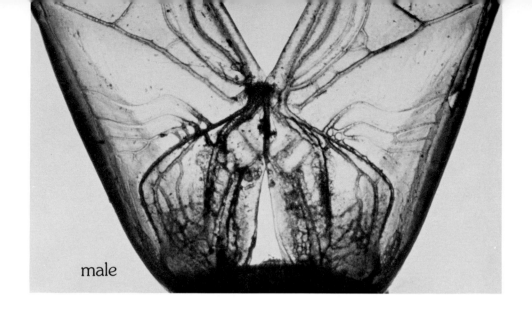

male

Male crickets can chirp because the veins in their wings are specially thickened and shaped to make sounds when rubbed together.

The simple veins of the females' wings cannot produce sound.

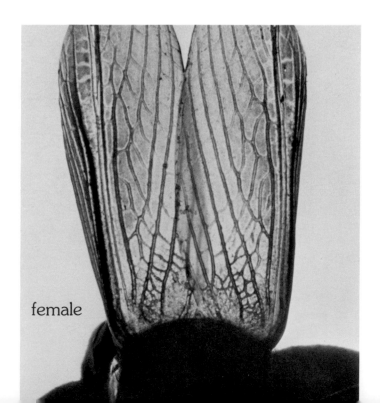

female

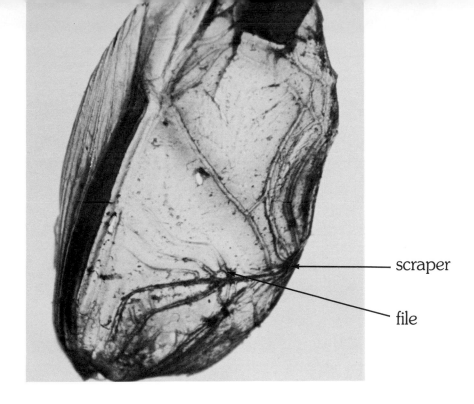

scraper

file

One vein on the male's wing has ridges on it. This vein is the "file." A smaller ridge at the edge of the wing is called the "scraper." When the scraper of one wing rubs against the file of the other, it makes a chirping sound.

Perhaps the most amazing thing about a cricket's song is how loud it is. How can such tiny veins make a chirp that can be heard across a field? The answer is that the file and scraper set the wings vibrating, and they act as amplifiers to magnify the sound. If the part of the wings above the file and scraper is removed, a cricket will still chirp, but the sound cannot be heard.

Crickets have several songs, which send different messages to other crickets.

The one heard most often is the *calling song*. Male crickets stay in one place and make a series of high musical chirps. This song attracts females and tells other males to keep away. In this way, each male stakes out his own territory.

If another male comes too close, the first cricket changes to the *rivalry song*—especially long, loud chirps. If the other cricket doesn't leave, the pair may fight, lashing each other with antennae, sparring with forelegs, biting with mandibles, and even butting each other like goats.

Such aggression is seen more often in field crickets than house crickets. In either case, however, one male usually backs off after a while, and the calling song is heard once again.

33

A female that is ready to mate turns so that the male's
calling song is received by the ears on her forelegs.
Then she walks forward, keeping the sound centered
between the ears. In this way, she can find the male
even if he is too far away to see.

When the female gets close, the male's chirping changes to the *mating song*, which is faster and softer. When she hears this song, the female walks up onto the male's back.

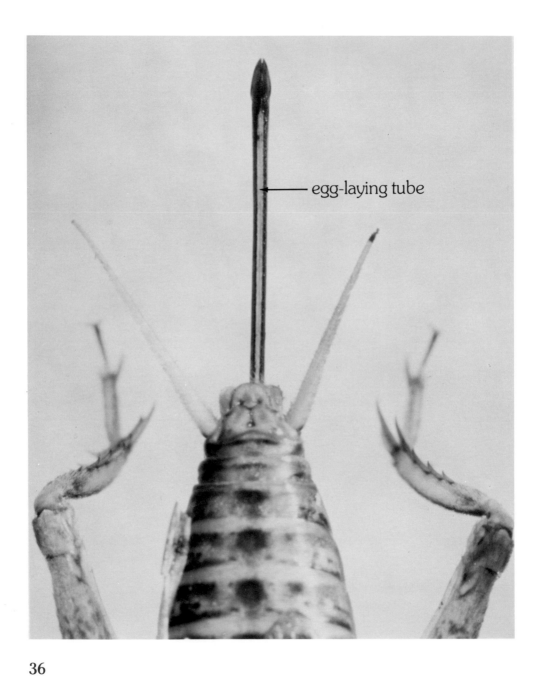

egg-laying tube

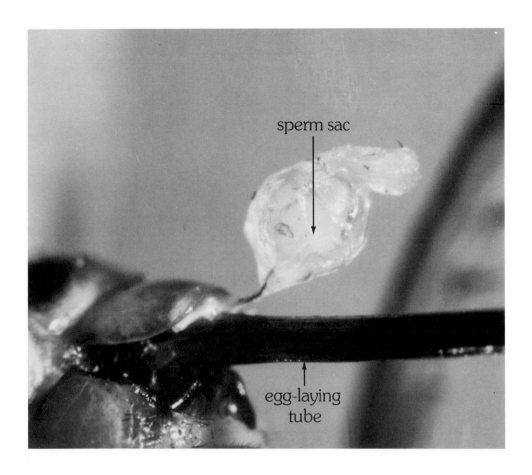

sperm sac

egg-laying
tube

With the tip of his abdomen, the male inserts the tube
of a sperm sac into an opening near the female's egg-
laying tube. This sac stays in place for an hour or so
after mating, until the sperm have entered the female's
abdomen. There they will fertilize the eggs inside
her body.

38

The female lays her eggs by inserting her egg-laying tube into damp sand. Sense organs in her palpi and egg-laying tube tell her whether the soil is moist enough. If it is too dry, the cricket postpones laying the eggs and looks for another place.

This close-up picture shows a single egg just as it is being released from the egg-laying tube.

Eggs before hatching

Emerging cricket

Many baby insects look very different from their parents. Caterpillars, for example, look nothing like their parents, adult moths. After a period of growing, the young enter a resting stage in a cocoon and develop into adults. This kind of change is called metamorphosis.

Crickets and many other insects do not have complete metamorphosis. When the eggs hatch, the baby crickets look like miniature models of their parents, except that they do not have wings and cannot mate. They have no resting stage. Instead, they grow larger and larger until they reach adulthood.

Baby cricket three hours after hatching

Each time the young cricket has a spurt of growth, it finds itself crowded into a too-small skin. This is because the insect's exoskeleton is made of nonliving material and cannot expand or grow. This old skin must be shed. As a new skin grows under the old one, a special chemical weakens the old skin by dissolving its inner layer. Finally the insect splits the outer layer apart and emerges. This process is called molting.

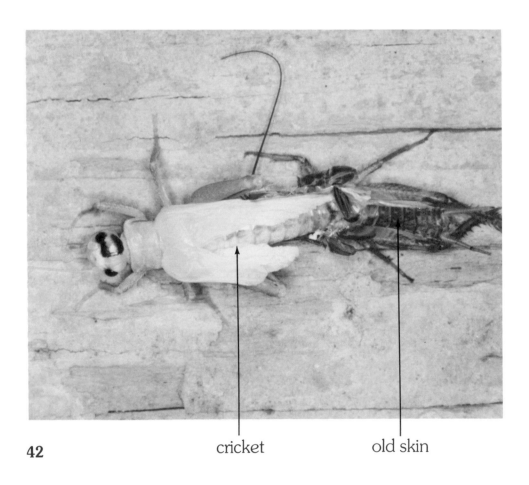

cricket   old skin

The newly molted insect seems to grow larger in a few seconds. Actually it is not growing—it has already done that inside the old shell. It is really stretching out and expanding after having been squeezed small inside the old skin.

At first the new skin is soft and white. In a few hours, it hardens and grows darker, until it is the same color as the old skin.

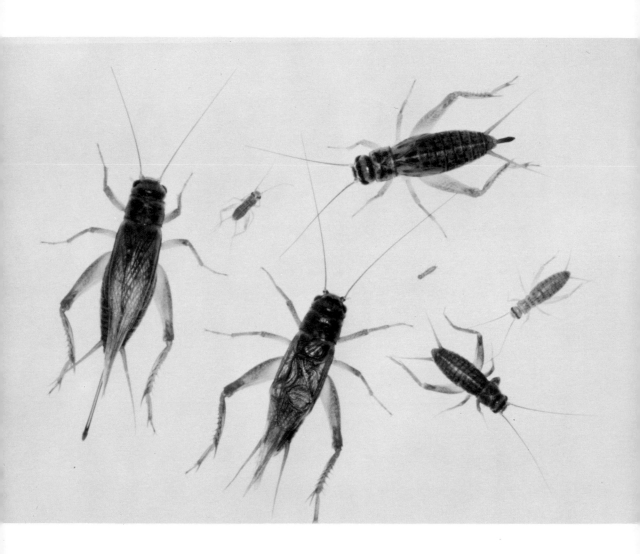

A young cricket molts eight to ten times before becoming an adult.

After the sixth or seventh molt, we can see the beginnings of wings.

Before the last molt, the body of the adult insect, with wings and reproductive organs, forms under the old skin. When the skin is shed, the full-grown insect emerges—tiny, intricate, and fully equipped for survival.

About the Author

Born in Newark, New Jersey, JOANNA COLE grew up in East Orange. After attending the University of Massachusetts and Indiana University, she earned a B.A. degree in psychology at the City College of New York. Later she took graduate courses in elementary education at New York University and served for one year in a Brooklyn elementary school as a teacher and librarian. A former editor, Mrs. Cole now devotes herself full time to writing. She lives in New York City with her husband and daughter.

About the Photographers

JEROME WEXLER was born in New York City, where he attended Pratt Institute. His interest in photography started when he was in the ninth grade. After service in World War II, he worked for the State Department in Europe as a photographer. Since then he has illustrated many children's books with his photographs of plants and animals. He lives with his wife in Madison, Connecticut.

RAYMOND A. MENDEZ was born in New York City. He combines his love of nature with his artistic training in a free-lance business that includes model making, animal wrangling, and nature photography. His photographic work has been published in *Natural History, Discover,* and *Geo* magazines, as well as a variety of books.